MW01291780

KNOWING THE
PEACE OF GOD

DR. THERON D. WILLIAMS

CHURCH DIGEST BOOKS
INDIANAPOLIS, IN

PRESS

Knowing The Peace of God
by Dr. Theron D. Williams

Printed in the United States of America

ISBN 978-1-60647-136-4

Dr. Theron D. Williams
Church Digest Books
P.O. Box 26087
Indianapolis, IN 46226

www.xulonpress.com

Contents

Chapter 1

Introduction

I had been working in my office for hours. I took a break and stretched. During the stretch, I felt a sensation akin to a water balloon bursting in my chest. The pain of it literally brought me to my knees. Immediately afterwards, I started burping. I thought I had a bad case of indigestion. It is not unusual for me to have gas bubbles in my chest; in fact, one time I had thought I was having a heart attack and was rushed to the hospital, only to find that it *had* been gas. I thought something similar was happening now. I started explaining to myself why it couldn't be a heart attack. I reminded myself of how healthy my lifestyle was: I exercise daily, eat the right foods, don't smoke, drink a glass of red wine daily — I had done the right things.

I got off the floor, got into my car, and drove home. When I got out of my car, I felt a sharp pain in my lower back and down my right leg. I limped into my house. Again, I told myself that everything was fine; I had just increased my exercise routine and thought I had simply strained myself. I figured if I could rest for a week or two, I'd be okay. The next day I felt intense pain running up my neck and into the back of my head. Still, I refused to believe that something was seriously wrong with me.

The next day, however, I went to church and ended up preaching sitting down instead of standing up, because I was in so much pain. I preached the first service but couldn't do the second. I went to the doctor later that day. He diagnosed me with an inflamed sciatic nerve, gave me pain medication, and told me to rest. After a couple of weeks, I went to my primary care doctor, who confirmed the previous doctor's diagnosis. He told me I could resume my exercise when I felt better. For the next five months, it was business as usual.

After five months, I tried to resume my workout, which included swimming. I swam half a length and my heart started to flutter. I went to see my doctor, who examined my heart; he told me he didn't like what the test showed and recommended a cardiologist.

I went to preach a revival the following week and then went on vacation. When I returned home, I kept my appointment with my cardiologist for a stress test. I was hooked up to the heart machine. The technician left the room during the exam to get the cardiologist. The doctor gave me the terrible news that I had an aneurysm, a dissected aorta, and leaking heart value. She told me that 98 percent of the people who have similar experiences die almost instantly—but I'd had these ailments for five months.

The surgery was scheduled for a Wednesday afternoon. My congregation, family, friends, and other church members around the country prayed for me. The surgery, which usually takes eight hours, ended up taking thirteen hours. I recuperated in the hospital for thirteen days. I went home and recovered. I reassumed my pulpit after three months.

By studying my injuries, I came to realize how serious they were. I became full of fear and anxiety over my future. Above everything else, I wanted peace in my life—not money, fame, fortune, popularity, a megachurch, or any of the other things that I had thought were important before my surgery. I just wanted peace of mind, which seemed almost unattainable.

But then I turned to the Word of God. I had been preaching at the same church for almost twenty years. In sermons I had told my congregation that peace could be found in God in any and all situations. It was my turn to be in a situation in which I had to rely totally on God, because peace and security were not going to come from any place else.

The most exciting book in the Bible for me is the book of Philippians. To know that the apostle Paul was in jail when he wrote this epistle and to read its radiant positivity makes this epistle even more intriguing. Paul's words in 4:8–10 set me on the path to knowing the peace of God in my situation. I am sure that whatever you are going through this passage will bring you, too, to know the peace of God.

Finally, brethren, whatever is true, whatever is honorable, whatever is just, whatever is pure, whatever is lovely, whatever is admirable, if there is any excellence, if there is anything worthy of praise, think about these things. What you have learned and received and heard and seen in me, do; and the God of peace will be with you. (NIV)

—Philippians 4:8–10

Chapter 2

Life's Ultimate Goal

The ultimate goal in life is to secure the feeling that peace and happiness bring us. All of us are after this wonderful feeling. In a real sense, the acquisition of this feeling is the bottom line of everything we do, whether we are aware of this idea or not.

If you ask yourself a series of "then what" questions, you'll be surprised that at the end of all that you aspire to do, you'll end with the statement *Then I'll be happy, satisfied, or at peace.* How many times have you said, "I'll be so happy when I pay off these bills"? It is not that the bills are creating the problem—it is that your bills are blocking you from happiness. So happiness is really what you want. How many parents have you ever heard say, "I'll be glad when these kids grow up and are out of the house"? The kids, as they see them, are blocking them from happiness; therefore, happiness is really what they want. "I'm getting out of this marriage because I'm not happy," people often think. Happiness is what these people are after; as they view it, the marriage is blocking them from happiness. The bottom line of all our endeavors is the conscious or unconscious pursuit of peace and happiness.

A man lived on one of the beautiful African islands. He spent three mornings each week fishing and gathering fruits and vegetables. He spent his afternoons playing with his beautiful wife and children and spent his evenings with friends and family members. He continually experienced feelings of happiness, peace, serenity, and satisfaction.

Businessmen from the West came to visit the beautiful island where this peaceful man lived. They saw his ingenious method of fishing and immediately realized how much money they could make in their Western market by using this technique. They approached the peaceful man, introduced themselves, and explained to him that his fishing method, if marketed correctly, could make a lot of money, thus enhancing his quality of life. The peaceful man asked, "How could this be done?"

The men explained, "First you'll have to patent the idea," to which the man asked, "And then what?"

The businessmen continued, "And then we'll find some investors, so that we may purchase the equipment we are going to need."

The peaceful man asked, "And then what?"

"We'll hire a staff and start fishing."

"And then what?" he asked.

"Then we'll distribute seafood to outlets around the world."

The peaceful man again asked, "And then what?"

"We'll take the business public and sell stock!"

The islander calmly asked, "And then what?"

"Then you'll be a rich man."

"And then what?"

"You can have cars, clothes, houses, planes and travel the world."

"And then what?"

"You can retire."

"And then what?"

"You can buy your own little island where you can fish; eat fruits and vegetables; spend time with your children, wife, family and friends; and live in peace and happiness."

The peaceful man responded, "Why go through all of that trouble when I already have what you are saying I'll end up with?"

As I mentioned before, the ultimate goal of all our endeavors is to secure the feeling of peace and happiness, although most of us do not know this about ourselves. When we come to recognize this, however, the realization will change our entire approach to life.

Ironically, people stress themselves out trying to secure the feeling of peace. People have worried themselves into early graves, pursuing that elusive feeling of peace and happiness. We worry about our children, money, careers, relationships, and many other things, because subconsciously we believe that when those things turn out the way we think they should, we will have peace and happiness. We pray that our children do well in school, go to college and graduate, get a good job or start a business, settle down and marry the ideal person, raise children, teach them the ways of God, and live happily ever after. We want this for our children because we love them, but also because we want feelings of peace and happiness from knowing our children are prospering.

We pursue money so that we can purchase certain necessities and luxuries in life that bring us happiness and peace. We pursue certain careers because we believe that a particular job will bring us the feelings associated with peace and happiness. We find our soul mates and want to settle down and marry, because we conclude that this is the person who gives us the feeling of happiness, peace, and wholeness.

Jeannette Maw, editor of the online magazine *GoodVibe,* wrote a very enlightening article entitled "Eliminate the Middleman" that best explains our ultimate pursuit of happiness:

> There are two foundational questions that everyone should consider when trying to determine what one really wants; they are, "what do you want," and why do you want it?" Take a moment to reflect on those two questions. What do you want, and why do you want it? Some might say, "I want to find the perfect house because it will give me more peace." Or maybe, "I want to drop a couple pounds because I want to feel good about how I look." Or perhaps, "I want to reduce my work and increase my income because

that will allow me to enjoy life more." What we're really after is how we think that thing or experience or person is going to make us feel. So what do you say we drop the middleman, huh? Let's go direct! When we identify the **real** target we're *much* more likely to succeed. I mean, how many times have you (or someone you know) gotten the thing you thought you wanted, but afterwards felt let down or unfulfilled? Like, we drop ten pounds, but once we get there, we just think we need to drop five more before we're satisfied? Or we get the relationship we said we wanted, but after the newness wears off, we still feel empty inside? Or we achieve our career success, but instead of being thrilled we're just worn out? That's because we were shooting for the first thing (what we want) when we really wanted the second (why we want it; that is, the feeling we think it will give us). (GoodVibe Coaching, Dec. 18, 2007). Jmaw@goodvibecoaching.com

I used to underestimate feelings by thinking of them as something fleeting and therefore unimportant. However, feelings are important, because they are barometers that alert us to where we are in our alignment with God. The state of happiness is the intended state in which God designed us to live. Everything Adam and Eve needed to perpetuate this state of happiness was attainable when they lived in the Garden of Eden. When you feel good, peaceful, or happy, these feelings indicate that you are in alignment with God. When you feel bad, ill at ease, or troubled, those feelings indicate you are further away from divine alignment.

If that is true, was Jesus out of divine alignment when, in John 12:27, He said: "Now my heart is troubled, and what shall I say? 'Father, save me from this hour?' No, it was for this very reason I came to this hour"? In this text, Jesus contemplated not going through with the crucifixion, which was His divine purpose. The very thought of His being out of alignment with the will of God created a troubled spirit. Feelings help us determine if we are in alignment with God. When we feel bad, anxious, or troubled, we know it's time for a divine realignment.

In Matthew 6:24–36, Jesus teaches that feelings such as anxiety and worry are indicators of our misalignment with God:

> This is why I tell you: do not be worried about the food and drink you need in order to stay alive, or about clothes for your body. After all, isn't life worth more than food? And isn't the body worth more than clothes? Look at the birds: they do not plant seeds, gather a harvest and put it in barns; yet your Father in heaven takes care of them! Aren't you worth much more than birds? Can any of you live a bit longer by worrying about it? And why worry about clothes? Look how the wild flowers grow: they do not work or make clothes for themselves. But I tell you that not

even King Solomon with all his wealth had clothes as beautiful as one of these flowers. It is God who clothes the wild grass that is here today and gone tomorrow, burned up in the oven. Won't he be all the more sure to clothe you? What little faith you have! So do not start worrying: "Where will my food come from? Or my drink? Or my clothes?" (These are the things the pagans are always concerned about.) Your Father in heaven knows that you need all these things. Instead, be concerned above everything else with the Kingdom of God and with what he requires of you, and he will provide you with all these other things. (GN)

The pagans referred to in this text represent those who are out of alignment with God. These are the ones who often experience anxiety and worriment. This is not so for the children of God, because their only job is to stay in alignment with Him. The birds and the flowers don't worry about these things, because nature is in harmony with God; and when you are in harmony with God, you don't worry either. The suggestion is to get attuned to God's will. When you are in alignment with God, you attract the very things that those misaligned with God lack and worry about; that's why Jesus said that these things "shall be added unto you."

One day I was having trouble with my car. Whenever I drove faster than fifty miles an hour, the front end shook violently. Even at low speeds, I had to fight the steering wheel to keep the car going straight. I took the car to a mechanic, who told me that the front wheels were out of alignment and that I needed a front-end alignment.

Where there is peace, trouble cannot persist. Trouble and peace cannot occupy the same space at the same time. It is like light and darkness: darkness vanishes with the presence of light. Jesus says in John 14:27: "Peace I leave with you; my peace I give you. I do not give to you as the world gives.. Do not let your hearts be troubled and do not be afraid." When the peace of God is present, trouble and fear must leave. The only time trouble and fear enter our lives is when peace is absent—and the only time peace is absent from our lives is when life is not in alignment with God. We must pay attention to our feelings because they are important.

Since you now understand that what we really want is the feeling engendered by peace and happiness, how would you feel if you knew you could possess that feeling without having to go into debt, thinking that you could *buy* this feeling of peace? What if you could obtain that feeling without assuming a huge mortgage, obsessing over expensive cars that you really don't need, or maxing out your credit cards by shopping? What if you could get feelings of peace and happiness for *free*?

Chapter 3

Think on These Things

Paul encourages his audience to think on the seven virtues that he points out in Philippians 4:8, that are designed to bring the peace of God into their lives." In this passage, *to think* means far more than simply to give these virtues a passing glance or merely allowing them to cross your mind. Paul had in mind something much more profound. Different translations of this passage help us to understand the impact of his idea *to think:*

New Living Translation: "Fix your thoughts on what is true."

Good News Translation: "Fill your minds with those things."

The Complete Jewish Bible: "Focus your thoughts on what is true."

Weymouth New Testament: "Cherish the thought of these things."

New American Standard Bible: "Dwell on these things."

We cannot be sure which translation most accurately conveys Paul's idea, but we do know that when he uses the term *think,* he means more than just a fleeting thought concerning these virtues. Let's briefly examine each of these five translations.

The New Living Translation says, "Fix your thoughts." If this is the most accurate translation, it refers to directing all of one's attention for an indefinite period of time on these virtues. The word *fix* also implies permanence, meaning that these virtues are a permanent part of one's thought process.

When our congregation moved into our new church edifice, we affixed to the building the name "Mount Carmel Baptist Church," and it became a permanent part of the building. Since then, we have had many signs on and around the building, but they were not fixed. We have had signs on and around our building advertising enrollment for our Christian academy, vacation Bible school, spring revival, fall revival, and other events. These signs were seasonal; therefore, they were removed after the event was over. These signs were temporary. The name of the church, however, will always be on the building, because it is permanent.

The emphasis is to make these virtues a permanent part of one's thoughts.

The Good News Translation tells us, "Fill your minds." This means to purposefully fill your mind with these virtues. The books we read, the conversations in which we engage, the TV programs we watch, the music we listen to—what we consciously meditate on will fill our minds. We have to make beneficial deposits into our minds, because what we deposit into our minds is what will manifest in our lives.

The Complete Jewish Bible says, "Focus your thought"; that is, to make these virtues the center of your thoughts and to meditate upon them. This has more to do with the act of meditation than do the other translations. Meditation is making conscious contact with God. While you are making conscious contact with God, you are centering your thoughts on these virtues.

The Weymouth New Testament says, "Cherish the thought of these things." This means to devote yourself to these virtues and protect them lovingly by not allowing them to be replaced with negative thoughts. It has been estimated that over thirty thousand thoughts pass through our minds every day. Other thoughts often replace the thoughts of these virtues, so they need to be lovingly protected.

The New American Standard Bible says, "Dwell on these things." That means we are to become so comfortable with these virtues that we literally make ourselves at home in them. Not only do these virtues live in us, but we are to also live, or dwell, in these virtues.

Origin of Thought

Our thoughts come from a deep internal reservoir of experiences that we have built up over time. Human beings are born with no innate or built-in mental content—we are born as "blank slates"—and humans' entire resource of knowledge is accumulated from their experiences and sensory perceptions of the outside world. Human thoughts then emerge from the soul.

We must now consider the function of the soul in relationship to the spirit and body. According to Genesis 2:7, man is made up of only two elements, spirit and flesh. But when God fused the two together, they produced a third dimension called soul. The tripartite make-up of man is body, soul, and spirit. The function of the body is to bring us in contact with the material world. Through our sense of touch, taste, sight, hearing, and smell, we are brought into world-consciousness. The soul is comprised of intellect, mind, reasoning, and knowledge; it is the seat of personality—it's who we are. The soul brings us into self-consciousness. The spirit is the part by which we have communion with God. It is only through the spirit that we can apprehend and worship God. God dwells in our spirit. So the spirit brings us into God-consciousness. The triune make-up of man is like a light bulb. The bulb itself is the body, the internal wiring is the soul, and the actual electricity that flows through it is the spirit.

Which one of the three is running the show: the spirit, the body, or the soul? Which part is in control of your life? All three are jockeying for supremacy in your life. Some people allow the flesh to have supremacy. When flesh has supremacy in your life, you are led through life by your appetite. As Paul writes in Philippians 3:19, "whose end is destruction, whose belly is their God." (KJV). In the Bible, the word *belly* is often a metaphor for "appetite." Paul contends that one's end will be destruction whenever one allows one's appetite precedence over God. The person who allows flesh to have supremacy follows the dictates of his desires. That person's life is lived according to the pleasure principle; that is, if it feels good, do it.

If the soul is in control, however, then the ego has the upper hand. Ego is the part of the psyche that gives us ideas about who we are. The ego never tells you who you really are but gives a false sense of yourself. the ego is a false self created by unconscious identification with things.

If the word *ego* could be used as an acronym, it would stand for easing God out. We all have our own ego, and it's quite useful at times; but when we allow it to have supremacy, it disconnects us from God. Wayne Dyer, noted psychologist and best-selling author, has suggested that when ego has supremacy in our lives, we'll know it, because it forces us to believe at least three false things about ourselves. It causes us to believe that:

We are what we do.
We are what we have.
We are what others think of us.

When we define ourselves on the basis of what we do, we mistakenly attribute value and worth to ourselves and others solely on things such as where we grew up, from which school we graduated, where we now live, and what we do for a living. Some people may have low self-esteem because of what they do for a living. People who work cleaning floors or flipping hamburgers may feel embarrassed because they do not have "prestigious" jobs. People may feel that way because ego has the upper hand in their lives and has convinced them that they are what they do.

A college classmate of mine went on to law school and graduated with honors. He landed an "important" job and made lots of money. He fell in love with a young woman and constantly bragged about her sense of style, her personality, and her physical beauty, but he broke up with her when he found out that she worked as a maid at a hotel. This man defined himself and others on the basis of what they did. His ego is in control of his life.

Ego also causes us to define ourselves by what we have. If someone has an abundance of material things, then that person is "somebody." But if someone has very little, then he is considered "nobody." The desire to be somebody by acquiring things is what drives many of us. When the stock market crashed on Black Friday in 1929, many rich people committed suicide because they had lost their money. They could not imagine living without their material things because they had defined themselves by their possessions.

People who are controlled by ego are overly attached to possessions, the work you do, social status and recognition, knowledge and education, physical appearance, special abilities, relationships, personal and family history, belief systems, and often also political, nationalistic, racial, religious, and other collective attachments. None of these is you.

Ego defines us by what others think of us. You will know that ego is in control when you are always looking for the approval of others. *How do I look to others? Does my boss like me? Will my spouse approve of me? Will my children love me? What will the church think of me?* If you are bombarded with this kind of thinking, ego has the upper hand.

In the past, when people accused me of acting a certain way that I knew wasn't true, I would argue with them to try to prove them wrong. I learned that that was my ego forcing me to attempt to convince my accusers otherwise, because I needed them to think of me in a way that affirmed who my ego told me I was. When you know who you really are—that is, when you are defined by God—what another person thinks about you will not add or subtract value from you.

I offered the following illustration to my church to teach that value comes from a higher power and not from the compliments or criticisms from people around you. I held up a twenty-dollar bill and asked the congregation, "How much is this twenty-dollar bill worth?" Of course, they all answered, "Twenty dollars."

I then pretended the twenty-dollar bill was a person and began to talk to it, complimenting it profusely in front of the congregation. I told the bill how much I loved its shade of green. I praised the picture of President Andrew Jackson on its front. I told him that he was the greatest president in U.S.

history. I told Andrew Jackson how much I admired the way he'd presided over the country and how he'd handled Congress and the courts. I praised his foreign and domestic policies. I continued for several minutes, heaping compliments on the twenty-dollar bill. Afterwards I held up the twenty-dollar bill and asked the congregation, "Now how much is the twenty-dollar bill worth?" They replied, "Twenty dollars." I then screamed insults at the twenty-dollar bill. I crumpled it up, threw it down on the floor, kicked it, and stomped on it. Then I picked it up and asked the congregation, "How much is it worth now?" By now they were laughing, because they had gotten the point. They responded, "Twenty dollars!"

True worth and value are not determined by compliments or criticisms. When one is ruled by one's ego, others are allowed to determine one's value, but when one is led by the spirit, it's clear that one's worth is determined by God. As long as the ego is in control of your life, you cannot be at peace or fulfilled except for short periods when you obtained what you wanted, when a craving has just been fulfilled.

Spirit is the highest and noblest of the three parts of man. The human spirit is not to be confused with the Holy Spirit. The human spirit is given to us at birth; the Holy Spirit is given at our new birth. The human spirit consists of three parts. They are conscience, intuition, and communion. The function of the conscience is to discern right from wrong. Intuition is that function of the human spirit that perceives truth independently of any reasoning process. Intuition means knowing something instinctively. Malcolm Gladwell, in his book *Blink,* calls the concept of intuition "the power of thinking without thinking." In this book, Gladwell tells an anecdote that occurred in the life of the multibillionaire J. Paul Getty concerning his desire to purchase what he thought was a valuable statue. He was prepared to pay almost ten million dollars for it.

Getty, a prudent businessman, had the statue examined by the top people in the art industry. After their lengthy investigations, they concluded that the statue was authentic. However, just before he purchased it, the Getty Museum was visited by noted Italian art historian Federico Zeri and Evelyn Harrison, the foremost expert on Greek sculptures. When she looked at the statue, Harrison instinctively knew that something was wrong with it. A new investigation was launched, and this time it was proved that the statue was a fake. She had what she called "an intuitive repulsion" of the statute. She knew something was wrong but did not know how she knew.[1]

The final function of the human spirit is communion with God. In fact, for the born-again believer, the Holy Spirit resides with the human spirit. When your soul gives the Spirit the upper hand in your life, the Spirit decides what you think. And you'll know that your thoughts are of the Spirit because your thoughts will bring life, hope, faith, and peace. If not, those thoughts are not of the Spirit.

---

[1] Malcolm Gladwell, *Blink,* (New York: Little, Brown and Company, 2005) p.3

Chapter 4

Think on Those Things That Are True
Philippians 4:8

The Greek translation of the word *true* in Philippians 4:8 is *ale‾the‾s*, meaning "to come into an awareness of a reality that is not concealed, hidden, or covered with falsehoods." In the text, Paul encourages his audience to come into the awareness of the truth about reality. Truth and reality are not synonymous. Truth is what actually is, but reality is what something seems or appears to be. One's perception is one's reality, whether the reality has basis in truth or not.

White-supremacy groups have their own reality that is not necessarily based on truth. They believe that all nonwhite people are intellectually, morally, physically, and spiritually inferior to white people. Although this is their perception of the world, their reality has no basis in truth. Some militant black groups espouse the idea that all white people are evil. These groups' ideology is their perception of reality; so, for them, it is real, but it has no basis in truth.

Human perception is far too flawed for it to be the sole barometer of the truth. I once was observing a presentation in a very important meeting. In the middle of the presentation, I yawned. The presenter interrupted his presentation and said to me, "Pastor, I don't mean to bore you, so why don't I wrap this up?" The presenter saw me yawn and through his flawed human perception concluded that I must be bored and that, therefore, he should rush through his presentation and thus release me from my boredom. My actions became his perceived reality, even though his reality had no basis in truth at all.

Yawning is not necessarily a sign of boredom. The truth is that yawning is a reflex triggered from the brain; yawning is simply the brain's way of trying to get oxygen. The truth is that I was very much interested in the presentation and that I thought the presenter was doing a fine job. But the presenter projected his reality onto me and responded on the basis of his flawed, "truthless" reality.

A father came in to my office to talk to me about his daughter, who was a senior in college. According to him, she had a problem that was getting out of hand. She perceived that everyone was out to get her. Her biology professor had advised the seniors that they should spend the Thanksgiving holiday on campus in the lab, preparing for their finals. Out of the two hundred twenty students in the class, she was one of thirty-two who decided to ignore her professor's request and go home for the holiday.

Upon her return to class, the professor gave a pop quiz. She got upset with the professor, accusing him of punishing her for going home for Thanksgiving by giving the class the pop quiz. Her father asked, "Did he give the pop quiz only to you or to the whole class? And how would he know if you had gone home?" She ignored the first question and answered, "Well someone must have told him that I went home; he doesn't like me, and he wants to flunk me!"

Her father viewed the online class syllabus, which showed a quiz scheduled for that day. It hadn't been a pop quiz after all. When he pointed out the quiz in the syllabus, she said, "Well, he didn't mention the quiz on the day of class before the holiday break; he just reminded us of the final. I know he is out to get me." She had formed her opinion of her professor on the basis of her perceived reality, which probably had no basis in truth.

People who think that someone is trying to do evil to them never experience peace. There are people who believe that based upon the misfortune in their lives, God doesn't love them or is out to hurt them. Often this paranoia extends to others: Their spouse has it in for them. Their co-workers, their fellow church members, their friends, and even strangers are planning to do them harm. One will never know the peace of God when all one experiences is reality based on perception. But there is a capacity in all of us to know the truth. Jesus said, "You shall know the truth, and the truth shall make you free." (John 8:34).

Paul appropriately begins his list of virtues by listing the virtue of truth first: "whatever is true." The other virtues will not bring one to know the peace of God if they are not received in truth. Truth creates the spiritual environment in which these other virtues can have their perfect work. Truth provides the foundation for these other virtues to stand.

The first thing a builder does when constructing an edifice is to lay the foundation. The foundation is the most important part of any building. The rest of the edifice is built on that foundation. For Paul, truth is the foundation upon which the other virtues rest.

Where Does Truth Begin?

Truth begins with the individual and his understanding of the truth about himself. In act 1, scene 3 of *Hamlet*, Polonius prepares his son Laertes for travel abroad in a speech in which he directs the youth to commit a "few precepts to memory." Among these precepts is this now familiar adage: "This above all: to thine own self be true / And it must follow, as the night the day / Thou canst not be false to any man." If one cannot be true to one's self, then it is impossible for one to be true to others or to God. But if one is true to one's self, one will find it easy to be true to others and to God. Who am I? Am I a human being who has spiritual experiences, or am I a spiritual being who has human experiences? The answer to this question determines if one is on the path to truth and self-knowledge or to falsehood and self-deception. If I define myself as a physical being that has spiritual experiences, I then place my physicality above my spirituality. The material takes precedence over the spiritual. My focus will mainly be on the physical domain.

If my focus remains in the physical domain, I will never know the peace of God. Jesus labeled those who overly concern themselves with materialism "pagans" or "nonspiritual." These are the people who place the physical above the spiritual — if they acknowledge the spiritual at all. Here are Jesus' words: "So do not worry, saying, 'What shall we eat?' or 'What shall we drink?' or 'What shall we wear?' For the pagans run after all these things, and your heavenly Father knows that you need them. But seek first his kingdom and his righteousness, and all these things will be given to you as well" (Matt. 6:31–33).

Viewing one's self primarily as a physical being that has an occasional spiritual experience is a self-view that has no basis in truth. The truth is that we are primarily spiritual beings who have physical experiences. Spirit was here first. In Genesis, when God created Adam, He formed him from the dust of the earth (physical) then breathed the breath of life (spirit) into him. Our spirit came directly from God. Since God was here before the earth was created, and since we were always a part of God, spiritually, we were in God before the earth existed.

Spirit existed before material and will remain when material has passed away. Spirit is eternal; material is temporary. We were spirit before we connected with the body, and we will be spirit when we depart the body. We are, therefore, spiritual beings who have physical experiences. When we come into the awareness of this foundational truth, we can know the truth about reality.

There are at least three truths that flow from our awareness of the truth about reality, truths that rescue us from stress and anxiety and bring us to know the peace of God. Wayne Dyer in his book, *Real Magic* describes these truths as follows: "I am a spiritual being; therefore, I am aware that I am never alone. I am a spiritual being; therefore, I am aware that God is at work in my life beyond mere cause and effect. I am a spiritual being; therefore, I have no room in my heart for grudges, hostility, and the need for revenge."

Spiritual beings are aware that they are never alone. God is with all of us all the time. Only those who are in the awareness of this truth benefit from the power and peace that God's presence provides. Living in this awareness allows us to know through our own personal experience with God that we are not alone. The only time we are afraid and anxious is when we lose the awareness of God's presence.

In the book of Genesis, Jacob dreamed of a ladder that reached up to heaven. Ascending and descending the ladder were angels. When Jacob awakened, he lamented, "God was in this place, and I wasn't aware of it!" (Genesis 28:16) In Psalm 23, David declared that he could even walk through the valley of the shadow of death without fearing something evil happening to him, because he was in the awareness that God was with him.

I am a spiritual being; therefore, I am aware that God is at work in my life beyond mere cause and effect. When God is at work in my life, I am aware that God can intervene at any time and suspend the rules of cause and effect.

In a cause-and-effect world, effects are always determined by previous causes. In fact, we can predict an effect by determining the cause. For example, if I jump off a twenty-five-foot building (cause), gravity is going to operate and pull me crashing to the ground (effect). If you have influenza and sneeze in my face and I ingest your virus (cause), I could catch the flu (effect).

The spiritual being, however, lives beyond mere cause and effect; therefore, his possibilities are not limited by cause and effect. Consider Paul's experience in the book of Acts:

> Once safely on shore, we found out that the island was called Malta. The islanders showed us unusual kindness. They built a fire and welcomed us all because it was raining and cold. Paul gathered a pile of brushwood and, as he put it on the fire, a viper, driven out by the heat, fastened itself on his hand. *When the islanders saw the snake hanging from his hand, they said to each other, "This man must be a murderer; for though he escaped from the sea, justice has not allowed him to live."* But Paul shook the snake off into the fire and

suffered no ill effects. The people expected
him to swell up or suddenly fall dead, but
after waiting a long time and seeing nothing
unusual happen to him, they changed their
minds and said he was a god.

—Acts 28:1–6, emphasis added

In this story, the islanders anticipated Paul to
swell up or fall dead (effect) because a venomous
snake had bitten him (cause). This spiritual man was
not totally subjected to the rules of cause and effect.
God suspended the cause-and-effect rule; therefore,
in spite of the cause, Paul suffered no ill effects.

In the Old Testament book of Daniel, the three
Hebrew boys were thrown into a fiery furnace. The
logical effect was for them to burn. But divine inter-
vention suspended the rules of cause and effect. The
Hebrew boys did not burn, not even a hair on their
heads.

In order for anyone to fully believe Jesus when
He said, "All things are possible," he cannot feel
bound to the cause-and-effect rule. If I subject myself
to the cause-and- effect rule, for me all things are
not possible, only those things that follow the rule of
cause and effect.

The spiritual world defies cause and effect. In
the spiritual world, things happen because God wills
them to, through our faith in Him. Moses led the children of Israel out of Egypt to the Red Sea. God parted
the waters and allowed the Israelites to pass through
safely. What could have caused this dramatic effect?

Those who are locked into the physical try to give a cause-and-effect explanation for this miracle. Simcha Jacobovici, an award-winning filmmaker, tries to give such an explanation of the parting of the Red Sea. He places the exodus at the time of the cataclysmic eruption of the volcano on the Greek island of Santorini, the linchpin to many of the theories proposed. Citing documented modern parallels, such as the 1986 Lake Nyos disaster in Cameroon, he believes that much of what the book of Exodus describes can be explained by a chain reaction of natural phenomena triggered by the Santorini eruption and a related earthquake. Furthermore, he contends that the biblical reference to the Red Sea is actually a mistranslation of an ancient Hebrew word that meant "Reed Sea," a now dried body of water. He hypothesizes that the seismic activity caused by the earthquake may have temporarily raised a land bridge for safe passage and that the pursuing Egyptians were the unfortunate victims of a tsunami approaching from the Mediterranean. Even if that is what caused the parting of the sea, how can people explain the perfect timing of these events?

The person who defines himself as a physical being that has spiritual experiences is subjected to the power of cause and effect. Recently I watched a Christian television program on which a minister recounted a miracle he had experienced he said: "I got a call in my office from a man whom I had never met before. He said he saw my broadcast on television in Europe and that he was moved to make a generous contribution into my ministry. He asked me to come over to Europe because he wanted to sign over the deeds of four condominiums to me. So I am leaving next week for Europe. Later I discussed the episode with a friend of mine, a fellow minister. He said, "Now what sense does that make? Nobody just gives away property like that. These ministers need to stop lying to people to raise money. Sooner or later, they will have to account for their behavior before God."

I asked, "So you don't believe someone would give away property for no apparent reason?"

"Heck, no! he responded." "If you believe that random acts of generosity on that scale do not happen unless precipitated by some tangible reward" I continued, "Then you are locked into a reality of cause and effect. For you, random acts of generosity will never happen because your perceived reality will block the possibility of them happening."

I am a spiritual being; therefore, I have no room in my heart for grudges, hostility, or revenge. How can I hold grudges, be hostile, or seek revenge if I believe that everything that happens in life is either divinely ordered or divinely approved? I thank God for everything and everyone who comes into my life. I recognize that God sends people and situations into my life for my own enhancement. That sickness, that troubled child, that nagging spouse, that mean, unreasonable boss, that irritating co-worker or fellow church member, as well as the good things that happen in my life, are all there to teach me and shape me into a better person. I like to refer to them, in the words of the late Dr. Frederick Samson, as "life's unwelcome tutors." Viewing life from this perspective, how can I harbor hostility, carry grudges, or seek revenge against anyone or anything? I know that everything that comes into my life is for my good. I am empowered to love those who perpetrate harm against me because I know that God will use it to enhance my own life in some way. Jesus was able to easily forgive Peter, who denied Him, and even those who crucified Him, because He understood that they were doing exactly what they were sent into His life to do. I know that at this very point in time in my life, I am supposed to be sitting in front of my computer typing the pages of this book. If that is true, then every situation and person that has come into my life thus far has attributed to my being here in this place at this time typing the pages of this book. The slightest alteration at any point in my life would have set me on a different path that would have prevented me from being in this place performing this task.

It is my opinion that we often prolong our time in uncomfortable situations because we fail to learn what God is trying to teach us from the situation. When God teaches us, it is not merely for intellectual enlightenment, but it is mainly for character or spiritual transformation. We convince God that we've gotten the point or learned our lesson, not by what we have learned cognitively, but by demonstrating to Him that what we have learned transforms our lives and makes us better people.

The 1993 comedy *Groundhog Day* starring Bill Murray dramatizes in a very powerful yet hilarious way how we get ourselves stuck in unpleasant life experiences because we refuse to learn the lessons that God is trying to teach. God cannot afford to promote you to a greater and more glorious life experience if you refuse to learn from the uncomfortable situation you are now in.

In this delightful movie, TV meteorologist Phil Connors; his producer, Rita; and cameraman, Larry; from the fictional Pittsburgh television station WPBH-TV9 travel to Punxsutawney, Pennsylvania, to cover the annual festivities with Punxsutawney Phil.

After the celebration concludes, a blizzard develops that Connors had predicted would miss them, closing the roads and shutting down long-distance phone service, forcing the team to return to Punxsutawney.

Connors awakens the next morning, however, to find it is again February 2, and his day unfolds in exactly the same way as before. He is aware of the repetition, but everyone else seems to be living February 2 exactly the same way and for the first time. This recursion repeats the following morning as well, over and over again.

For Connors, Groundhog Day begins each morning at 6 a.m., with his waking up to the same song, Sonny and Cher's "I Got You Babe," on his alarm clock radio. With his memories of the "previous" day intact, he is trapped in a seemingly endless time loop to repeat the same day in the same small town. After briefly trying to rationalize his situation and then thinking he is insane, Connors takes advantage of learning the day's events and the information he is able to gather about the town's inhabitants, realizing that his actions have no long-term consequences. He revels in this situation for a time: seducing beautiful women, stealing money, even driving drunk and experiencing a police chase.

He is able to befriend Rita and tells her of his circumstances, how he is reliving the day over and over again, and manages to convince her with his extensive knowledge of events to come, the lives of the Punxsutawney townspeople, and Rita herself. He opens his heart to Rita, and her advice helps him to gradually find a goal for his trapped life: as a benefactor to others. He cannot, in a single day, bring others to fulfill his needs, but he can achieve self-improvement by educating himself on a daily basis.

Eventually Connors is transformed from a jerk to a wonderful human being, which, in return, makes him an appreciated and beloved man in the town. Finally, after professing true love to Rita, one which she is able to accept, he wakes up on February 3. (Wikipedia).

God often uses life circumstances to transform us but we have to be conscious of the reality that God is ceaselessly working in our lives. It is only when we enter into this awareness that we can benefit and grow from life's circumstances.

Chapter 5

Think on Those Things That Are Honest
Philippians 4:8

The first of these virtues that Paul encourages his audience to think about are the things that are true. Truth provides the foundation for the other virtues that Paul lists in this passage. The second of these virtues is honesty. Honesty is applied truth. Honesty is truth in action. Truth must always precede honesty. Let's revisit Shakespeare's quote in Hamlet: "To thine own self be true / And it must follow, as the night the day/ Thou canst not be false to any man." Honest dealings with others are possible only if truth first prevails. Proverbs 12:27 states, "A truthful witness gives honest testimony, but a false witness tells lies." Here, truth precedes honesty. The witness can be honest only if the witness knows the truth. It is impossible for the lying witness to be honest because he does not speak the truth—only falsehood.

While truth precedes honesty, lies precede dishonesty. Dishonesty is applied lies. Dishonesty is a lie at work.

A salesman once tried to talk me into purchasing an expensive designer watch. The watch looked authentic, but I wanted to take the watch to a professional jeweler before I bought it. The salesman refused to allow me to have the jeweler examine it. His refusal suggested to me that the watch was a fake.

The salesman was not the manufacturer of the watch, so he didn't create the fake. However, he was aware that this was not an authentic watch and attempted to sell it to me as if it were. He applied his lie by attempting to pass a fake watch off as real; therefore, his actions were a form of dishonesty.

The fake watch was not the problem; the problem was that the salesman tried to convey that the watch was authentic, while aware of its inauthenticity. Had he tried to sell me the watch but mentioned that the watch was a fake, he would have been honest, because honesty is applied truth.

Let's push this thought further. What if the salesman had told me the watch was a fake, we negotiated a price, and I purchased it, knowing it was not the real thing? If I wear the watch, am I as dishonest as the dishonest salesman? The answer: It depends on my intentions. If I wear the watch simply because I like it—no problem. But if my intention is to impress others or to convince others that the watch is real, I am just as dishonest as the salesman. Just as he tried to deceive me, I am now trying to deceive others. My dishonesty, therefore, is not based on the inauthenticity of the watch or my wearing the watch, but on my *intentions* for wearing the watch. Honesty boils down to what one intends to do with the truth.

When Paul invites his readers to think on "whatever things are honest," it is not a call for Christians to reflect on past acts of honesty, but rather a challenge to apply the truth in any and all future actions. Paul suggests that all Christians' intentions should be to apply the truth in any and all situations.

In my morning devotions, during the meditation period, I fix my thoughts on those things that are honest, meaning I contemplate applying the truth in all situations, from stopping at every stop sign on my drive to work to accurately recording my work hours on my time sheet. I do my job to the best of my abilities, whether my boss is there or not. I don't extend my lunch period or leave my job earlier than my scheduled time, nor do I deliberately dawdle when leaving to accrue more time on my time sheet. I don't take supplies from my job without permission. These are proper applications of honesty.

Since Proverbs 23:7 says, "As a man thinks in his heart, so is he," if I meditate on things that are honest, I'll become honest. There is a difference between performing honest deeds and being an honest person. Merely performing honest deeds is simply *doing*, but being an honest person is *being*.

When I become an honest person, stopping at stop signs is what I naturally do. Driving within the speed limit is what I naturally do when I am an honest person. I don't need police to supervise my driving behavior, and I don't need my boss watching over me to make sure I come to work on time, because "honest" is what I am and not merely what I do. When honesty is simply something that I do, I need supervision from authority to keep me honest.

It is impossible to know the peace of God if one is dishonest. Dishonest people live in a constant state of anxiety because they are always thinking their dishonesty might be discovered. Even a person who tries to impress others with a fake designer watch worries that someone will recognize that the watch is a fake.

Many people cannot have peace because they are stuck in a cycle of dishonesty. Say, for instance, you set your clock alarm to go off at 6 a.m. because the truth is that 6 a.m. is the time you need to awaken to get to work on time. But when the alarm rings at six, you purposely lie there for an extra twenty minutes. When you finally get up, you are in a frantic rush to get to work. You start your day off in stress and anxiety because you began your day by being dishonest with yourself. Applying the truth in this context means getting up at six o'clock because you are aware of how much time it takes you to get to work.

But instead, you rush and stress. Your drive to work is anything but peaceful, because you are exceeding the speed limit; in this you are dishonest, because applied truth in this case equates to driving the speed limit. Speeding causes more tension because you are constantly watching for the police and trying to avoid being ticketed for speeding, and you have all the stress that goes along with it. You arrive at work ten minutes late, so you spend the day worried, wondering if anyone is going to find out that you are being dishonest about your arrival time.

You didn't get a chance to have breakfast this morning, so you leave a few minutes early for lunch. While at lunch, you cannot peacefully enjoy your food because you are concerned that someone knows you left early for lunch; thus, your lunch gives you indigestion.

At the end of the workday, you are emotionally drained, but you'd promised your significant other some time alone. But you think you need a drink to "take the edge off"; you're not really up to it tonight. So what do you do? You call home and lie by telling your significant other that you have to work late and will not be able to make it. Instead, you go to happy hour with your friends.

Your dishonesty causes you to worry. You ask yourself: *What if my significant other comes in and sees me? What if a friend comes in? Will my lie be discovered?* You down too many drinks too fast; now you're drunk, but you can't stay there long enough to sober up because you've got to get home because you were supposed to be at work.

Now you are driving under the influence — dishonesty leading to more tension. Your drive home is more stressful than ever, because you are well aware of the consequences of drunk driving. You are on guard for the police while thinking: *What if I hit a pedestrian or a car? What if I kill someone? Or what if someone runs into me, and the police show up and give me a Breathalyzer? I'll go to jail!* You make it home without incident, but you feel more tension because you were dishonest with your mate.

Now you must be careful and guarded in what you say because you don't want to give away where you really were. Not only that, but you must act as if you are sober! You just went a whole day without experiencing the peace of God, because, when dishonesty is present, there can be no peace.

If you are like most parents, you notice details about your kids. My oldest son has hands and fingernails like mine. My fingernails grow fast, and they can get very long if I allow it. My son allows his fingernails to grow to what he calls "scratching length." When he was a student in high school, I would ask him when he got home from school, "Do you have homework?" The answer was always, "I did it at school." I would ask, "Do you have any tests to study for?" The answer: "Yes, but I studied in study hall today." Question: "How are your grades?" Answer: "Real good. All A's and B's, except for a C in math."

The closer report-card time came, however, the more I would notice him biting his nails. For him, this was a sign of anxiety because he was anticipating bad grades because of missing homework assignments, low test scores, and lack of class participation. He created a stressful situation for himself by being dishonest.

If we are to know the peace of God, Paul says that we need to contemplate applying truth to all situations.

Chapter 6

Think on Those Things
That Are Fair
Philippians 4:8

What does it mean to be fair? And how does meditating, "fixing our minds," or contemplating fairness bring us to know the peace of God? Fairness is the condition of being free from bias, dishonesty, or injustice. Fairness is the state of being free from blemishes, imperfections. You cannot execute fairness unless you are fair in your essence. You have to be fair before you can demonstrate fairness. If fair is *what you are,* then your execution of fairness will come naturally.

To be fair you must first be free. It is interesting the order in which Paul lists these virtues. The preceding virtues influence the succeeding ones. To be free one must first know the truth, which is the first virtue on Paul's list. Christ said, "The truth shall make you free."

To be fair, we must be free from all biases and prejudices. To be free from these evils, we must control our egos. It is the ego that creates all our biases and prejudices. The ego provides an inaccurate perception about ourselves. It convinces us to believe that we are something or someone contradictory to who we truly are. It forces us to despise the authentic self and embrace the ego-created self.

The ego absorbs you into "self"; that is, the outer world, and convinces you of your own, what Wayne Dyer calls, separateness and specialness. He contends: "The feeling of separateness creates a competitive spirit. When I am convinced that I am separated from others and from material things and even from God, then I must compete with others to prove that I am better than others. If I'm better than others, then I have greater opportunity to acquire more material things than others, because *there is only so much stuff to go around.*"

We actually live in a competitive society. This is symptomatic of an ego-dominated culture that never ceases to remind us of our separateness. Everything is based on competition. In fact, there are built-in rewards for the "best" people. We have been taught from our earliest existence to compete. Siblings rival over everything from toys to parental attention. Children compete with their playmates to see who can run the fastest, who can throw the ball the farthest, who can hold their breath the longest.

This attitude carries over into scholastic achievements. The smartest high school students get the scholarships from the best schools. The best college students get the best intern opportunities. The best interns get the best jobs. The best employees get the most impressive promotions.

Competition fuels much of the corruption in business, religion, entertainment, sports, family, and education. The Enron scandal and others like it are the ugly symptoms of a competitive society. Billions of dollars were stolen from thousands of workers' pension funds. This money was divided among a few corporate crooks. Was this a contest between these thieves as to who could amass the most money? Or did their egos convince them that America's supply of money was going to run out so they had better get all they could by any means necessary?

Competition even rears its head in the church. Pastors compete with one another for the most members, for who can raise the most money, for who can preach the best sermon, for who can build the biggest and most impressive new church, for who can secure the most prestigious preaching engagements, for who can get the most speaking invitations. It has even reached a point where some congregations are taught that the measure of a successful ministry is determined by how many material things they can provide its minister. For example, a mega-church in the South bought its pastor a brand-new, expensive car for his twentieth pastoral anniversary. In response, the leaders of the *competing* church across town decided to purchase a car of equal or greater value for *their* pastor. What a way to spend the Lord's money!

In the entertainment industry, artists compete with one another for public support. Why should two artists compete with each other? A fan can only watch one movie at a time, listen to one song at a time, and attend one concert at a time. A fan has enough room in his heart to be equally loyal to many different artists. But ego tells these artists that they are separated from all others; therefore, they must prove they are better than others. Ego leads them to believe that they must be better in order to attract and keep a loyal fan base.

Performance-enhancing drugs are slowly taking the excitement out of sports. Some of the most high-profile athletes are guilty of using these drugs. Rather than pushing themselves to be their best, these athletes decide they must be better than the competition, even if it means taking drugs that put their careers and lives in jeopardy.

Sometimes the spirit of competition invades a marital relationship. I have a friend who has done well with his life, given his meager beginnings. He graduated from a prestigious law school and has an important job on Wall Street. Over the years, he has been awarded many honors and has garnered much public recognition and numerous awards. Every time he got a promotion or raise, however, his wife would become ill. Whenever he was to be honored for a special achievement, his wife would make an excuse as to why she couldn't attend the ceremony; or if she *did* attend, she would need to leave early, because of illness. She even got drunk at one of his recognition ceremonies and embarrassed them both.

During a marriage-counseling session, it was revealed that she was in fierce competition with him. She even competed with him for their children's affection. In her eyes, his success meant her failure, even though she benefited from his success. At one point, she cried: "I came from a better family than he, was raised in a better neighbor than he, made better grades in college than he, but look at him now—he is Mr. Everything, and I'm nothing. I guess you win; I can't compete with that." Ego had taught her that she was separate from her husband; competition, not cooperation, defined the marriage.

Ego also convinces us of our specialness. Since God created all of us, we have all been created equally. Therefore, if I am special, then either everyone else is also special or no one, including me, is special. There is no such thing as a select few special beings, while others are not.

People with specialness complexes think they are worthier than others; some believe they are God's favorites. If you are God's favorite, then we are all God's favorite. If you are not God's favorite, then neither am I. We are all the same in God's eyes.

I know people would like to believe their egos when their egos tell them that they are better than sinners and the unsaved. Ego has convinced the Bible-toting, Bible-quoting, church-going Christians that they are better than others who are not like them. Our real challenge, however, is not to be better than someone else, but to be better today than we were yesterday. God loves us all equally. Jesus said, "[God] causes his sun to rise on the evil and the good, and sends rain on the righteous and the unrighteous" (Matt. 5:45).

It is damaging when this specialness complex infiltrates a congregation. I have known people to become discouraged and frustrated with the church because they were told, in essence, that they were not special enough to be a part of the body of Christ. If they were not baptized in the right name, or if they didn't manifest certain spiritual gifts, or if they didn't embrace certain behaviors, they were excluded.

Christ simply said that the only requirement is to believe in Him. But the ego-driven desire to be special has caused us to follow other misleading criteria to become a part of the body of Christ. Remember, the acronym for ego is easing God out. We have eased out God's simple criterion for salvation and eased in our own.

Until we are free from the ego, we cannot be fair. Ego-driven biases and prejudices will prevent us from being fair. Jesus offered the basis for fairness when He urged, "Do unto others as you would them do unto you." Jesus was intimating that if you believe yourself to be special and expect to be treated a certain way, then you should treat others as if they are as special as you are.

Ego can be eliminated when you view everyone as you view yourself. If you think that it is dehumanizing for someone to yell at you, then you will not yell at others. If you think that it is disrespectful for someone to insult you, then you won't do it to others. If you think it is wrong for someone to judge you, then you won't judge others.

It is only when this divine principle can manifest in your life that you will be in a position to be fair. The more you meditate on things that are fair; that is, contemplate treating others as you would like to be treated, the more you will become a fair person.

Chapter 7

Think on Those Things That Are Pure
Philippians 4:8

T he Greek word for "pure" is *hagnos,* which means "free from any admixture of contaminants, taint, or filth." Any thought, therefore, can be a pure thought if it is free from the admixture of contaminants. Thoughts of sex, riches, power, and success that are usually associated with impurity can be changed to pure thoughts if they are free from contaminants.

Sexual thoughts are often incorrectly associated with sin and evil, because these thoughts are most often mixed with contaminating ideas. The concept of sex, however, is introduced early in the Bible — even before the concept of sin. As early as Genesis 2, sex is introduced: "For this reason a man will leave his father and mother and be united to his wife, and they will become one flesh." That is a blatant reference to sexual union between husband and wife.

In Genesis 13, the reality of wealth, power, and success were introduced through the story of Abraham. Riches, power and success were not considered inherantly evil until much later in Scripture when men begin to use their wealth and power to oppress and exploit the innocent.

When our thinking is contaminated it is always due to the introduction into our thinking one or more of the Seven Deadly Sins.

Seven Deadly Sins

The seven deadly sins, also known as the capital vices, or cardinal sins, are a group of vices that were originally used in early Christian teachings to educate and instruct followers concerning fallen man's tendency to sin. The Roman Catholic Church divided sin into two principal categories: *venial* sins, which were relatively minor and could be forgiven through any sacrament of the church, and the more severe *capital,* or *mortal,* sins, which, when committed, destroyed the life of grace and created the threat of eternal damnation unless absolved through either the sacrament of confession or through perfect contrition on the part of the penitent. The pervasiveness of the seven deadly sins as a theme among fourteenth-century European artists eventually helped to ingrain them in many areas of Christian culture and public consciousness throughout the world.

These seven deadly sins originate in our thoughts and then manifest in our actions. These are the thoughts that contaminate our thinking and render our thoughts impure. Any of these seven deadly sins, when mixed with our thinking, prevents us from having pure thoughts. Whenever our thoughts are impure, we cannot know the peace of God. When our thoughts are impure, it is because they are invariably admixed with one or more of the thoughts of the seven deadly sins.

Pride

The first of these deadly sins is pride. Pride is an inordinate opinion of one's own dignity, importance, or merit. Pride makes one think that one is more than he actually is. The Scriptures forbid this kind of thinking. Paul wrote to the Roman church, "For I say, through the grace given unto me, to every man that is among you, not to think of himself more highly than he ought to think." (Romans 12:3)

The truth is that we are all equal. There are some who make more money than others. Some people have more material possessions than others. Some have more glamorous and higher-profile jobs than others. Nevertheless, we are all equal. So, if you are special, then I am just as special. If you are not special, then neither am I. But pride causes us to think of ourselves as better than others, feeling entitled to preferential treatment. When we do not receive this treatment, we feel offended. And we cannot know the peace of God and the feeling of being offended at the same time.

I once was out to dinner with a popular musical artist. The waitress came to our table and took our drink orders. After the waitress left, the artist said: "I can't believe that she didn't recognize me! What kind of city is this where people don't know me?" I asked her, "Well, did you recognize her?" She answered: "No, why should I know her? Who is she, but a mere waitress?" I responded: "She is a human being who makes a living waiting tables, and you are a human being who makes a living singing. Why should you be offended that she doesn't recognize you? She doesn't seem to be offended that you didn't recognize her."

Our pride causes us to feel offended by others. If you don't expect preferential treatment from others, then it will be unlikely that you will be offended by others. The less you expect from others, the less likely you are to be offended by others. In fact, if you don't expect anything from anyone, you will feel grateful and appreciative when someone *does* treat you well, because you weren't expecting it.

Pride contaminates our thinking and renders our thoughts impure because pride crowds God out of our thinking. Pride forced God out of King Belshazzar's thinking; as a result, he paid a tragic price. In the book of Daniel, chapter 5, Belshazzar threw a party for his dignitaries. In his pride, Belshazzar sent for the golden vessels that his father, Nebuchadnezzar, had taken from the holy temple in Jerusalem. Nebuchadnezzar had so much reverence for the holy things of God that he had locked those holy vessels away in a safe place to avoid defiling them.

But Belshazzar, whose pride moved God out of his thinking, drank wine from them, desecrating the holy things of God. At that point, a hand came out of nowhere and wrote on the wall, "Number, number, weight, divisions." "Number" meant that God had numbered the days of Belshazzar's kingdom. "Weight" meant he had been weighed on the scales and found to be too light (see Daniel 5:17–27).

Daniel further explained to Belshazzar:

> The Supreme God made your father Nebuchadnezzar a great king and gave him dignity and majesty. . . . But because he became proud, stubborn, and cruel, he was removed from his royal throne and lost his place of honor. But you, his son, have not humbled yourself, even though you knew all this. You acted against the Lord of heaven and brought in the cups and bowls taken from his temple. You, your noblemen, your wives, and your concubines drank wine out of them and praised gods made of gold, silver, bronze, iron, wood, and stone—gods that cannot see or hear and that do not know anything. But you did not honor the God who determines whether you live or die and who controls everything you do. That is why God has sent the hand to write these words. (TMSG)

Pride causes our thoughts to be impure. It corrupts our thinking because it causes us to hold on to the wrongs that others have perpetrated against us, thus preventing us from forgiving. If I hold a grudge, I cannot experience the peace of God. It takes humility to admit when I am wrong and even greater humility to beg forgiveness from the person I transgressed.

It is rare for someone to ask forgiveness out of a true sense of contrition. Think back over your life. Count the times you have been wronged by others. Now count the people who have actually come to you and asked your forgiveness when they had nothing to gain by it. On the other hand, count the number of people you have wronged. To how many of those people have you gone and asked forgiveness?

Pride pollutes our thinking because it causes us to think that our point of view is superior to everyone else's. Pride exclaims: "Would everyone please shut up and listen to me? If everyone does as I say, then everything will work out just fine!"

Envy

Envy is the second of these deadly sins. Envy is the malignant desire for others' traits, status, or abilities. Because someone else has what we don't have, we develop anger, resentment, and even rage toward that person, the world, or even God. Because of our superiority complex, we are perplexed as to why someone else has certain things but we don't. In most instances, even when envious people have these things, they still tend to be upset when others have them, because they think no one but themselves is worthy of these things.

Envy pollutes our thinking because envious thoughts keep us in the attack mode. The envious tend to attack others for having, being, or doing more than they. This is extremely important to the envious, because they define people solely on the basis of external realities. They define others by their cars, houses, salaries, bodily appearance, clothes, education, etc. They constantly seek out people who have more material things than they do and then make negative remarks about them. They spread gossip about people who are more successful than they. They are critical of others' accomplishments and look for the negative in everything these people do.

They constantly hope for the failure or collapse of successful people, because they view everyone as a rival. They view life as a contest and everyone as their competitor. Therefore, they think it is their duty to pull down others that they view as ahead of them and keep down others that they view as beneath them. It is impossible to know the peace of God with thoughts of envy contaminating our thinking.

Envy is the fear of being replaced. People who are envious constantly watch those who they believe have the capacity to replace them, whether it's an employee or a significant other, or in some other area of life. The envious often attack those with these capacities.

In Matthew 2, King Herod was so evil that he ruled by intimidation and instilling fear in his subjects. When Christ was born, Herod found out that the child was hailed the new king. Herod's fear was of being replaced as king. He was more afraid of losing his position as king than of losing the affection of the people. Consider the following passage:

Now when Jesus was born in Bethlehem of Judaea in the days of Herod the king, behold, wise men from the east came to Jerusalem, saying, Where is he that is born King of the Jews? For we saw his star in the east, and are come to worship him. And when Herod the king heard it, he was troubled, and all Jerusalem with him. And gathering together all the chief priests and scribes of the people, he inquired of them where the Christ should be born. And they said unto him, In Bethlehem of Judaea: for thus it is written through the prophet, "And thou Bethlehem, land of Judah, art in no wise least among the princes of Judah: For out of thee shall come forth a governor, who shall be shepherd of my people Israel." Herod privily called the wise men, and learned of them exactly what time the star appeared. And he sent them to Bethlehem, and said, Go and search out exactly concerning the young child; and when ye have found him, bring me word, that I also may come and worship him. . . . . Now when they were departed, behold, an angel of the Lord appeareth to Joseph in a dream, saying, Arise and take the young child and his mother, and flee into Egypt, and be thou there until I tell thee: for Herod will seek the young child to destroy him. (NIV).

Although King Saul was not afraid of being replaced by David as king, he feared that David would replace him in the hearts of the people. Saul wanted his subjects to love him. David's threat to Saul was that David had the capacity to replace him in the affections of the people. Consider the following passage:

And it came to pass as they came, when David returned from the slaughter of the Philistine, that the women came out of all the cities of Israel, singing and dancing, to meet King Saul, with timbrels, with joy, and with instruments of music. And the women sang one to another as they played, and said, Saul hath slain his thousands, and David his ten thousands. And Saul was very wroth, and this saying displeased him; and he said, They have ascribed unto David ten thousands, and to me they have ascribed but thousands: and what can he have more but the kingdom? And Saul eyed David from that day and forward. And it came to pass on the morrow, that an evil spirit from God came mightily upon Saul, and he prophesied in the midst of the house: and David played with his hand, as he did day by day. And Saul had his spear in his hand; and Saul cast the spear; for he said, I will smite David even to the wall. And David avoided out of his presence twice. And Saul was afraid of David, because Jehovah was with him, and was departed from Saul. Therefore Saul removed him from him, and made him his captain over a thousand; and he went out and came in before the people. And David behaved himself wisely in all his ways; and Jehovah was with him. And when Saul saw that he behaved himself very wisely, he stood in awe of him. But all Israel and Judah loved David; for he went out and came in before them.

— 1 Samuel 18:6-12

Gluttony

Gluttony is the third of the seven deadly sins. It is an inordinate desire to consume more than one requires. Constant eating could be the result of a lack of faith in God to provide one's needs. Gluttony is often a reaction to the fear of lack or scarcity in one's life. Jesus comforts us in Matthew 6:31 by saying, "Don't worry about what you shall eat. . . . for your heavenly Father who feeds the birds of the air will take care of you." You can never experience the peace of God if you are worrying about lack in your life and engaging in gluttony.

Lust

Lust is an inordinate craving for the pleasures of the body. Lust focuses on pleasing oneself and often leads to unwholesome actions to fulfill one's desires, regardless of the consequences. Lust is about possession and greed. Lustful thoughts contaminate our thinking, because when under the influence of lust, we make all our decisions on the basis of our five senses. If it looks good, smells good, tastes good, feels good, or sounds good, it must be good. Thus to pleasure one's self becomes the ultimate goal.

To live for pleasure alone means that one has totally ignored the spiritual dimension of the self and is obsessed with the flesh. The Bible says, "But the widow who lives for pleasure is dead even while she lives" (1 Tim. 5:6). She is considered dead because she is living for the body only and has ignored her spiritual connection to God. We must live in an awareness of our connection with God. Death equates with existing in the absence of such awareness. When there is no awareness of our connection to God, the focus of our existence becomes the body. When the body becomes the focus, pleasuring the body becomes life's ultimate goal, and lust takes control.

When our minds are inundated with lustful thoughts, we look for things that are pleasurable to the eye. This is what got Eve into trouble in the Garden of Eden. She made a decision on the basis of the fruit's appearance. The Bible states, "When the woman saw that the fruit of the tree was good for food and pleasing to the eye . . ." (Gen. 3:6). When profound decisions are made solely on what is pleasing to your eye, your decisions are based on lust. Before important decisions are made, you must ask yourself, Is the decision based on lust?

I have known many a person who decided to marry an individual because the individual was very attractive. The only thing these people took into consideration was what was pleasing to the eye. Marriages basely solely on physical attraction are frequently short lived and often end in regret. A young man came to me for advice on buying a car. He had just graduated from college and was making close to forty thousand dollars annually at an entry-level accounting job. He had an apartment, student loans, and credit-card debt. He told me he saw a Hummer and was really smitten by it and had to have it. He had calculated his income and expenses and figured that, although it would be a tight squeeze, he could afford the monthly payments.

I asked him if he had considered the cost of gas and the Hummer's ridiculously low gas mileage. Had he thought about the cost to insure such a car and the cost of regular maintenance? But the car was so appealing to his eye that he took nothing else into consideration and purchased the car. Two years later, he was trying to sell it but couldn't, because he owed too much money on it and had negative equity. He regretted the purchase and admitted that that decision was based on lust.

To live a life motivated by lust is to view everything and everyone as a potential means to satisfy one's own selfish pleasures. Lustful thinking causes people to objectify others and uses them to satisfy personal pleasures. Lustful thinking relates to people as "I-it," rather than "I-you."

The booming pornography industry is symptomatic of our lust-based society. In pornography the models are objectified and exploited as mere means for others' sexual pleasure. Pornography contaminates thinking because the viewer sees the models as nothing more than sexual objects. And in time, the viewer will begin to evaluate people on the basis of what kind of sexual object they can become. Lustful thinking pollutes our thinking because it causes us to relate to others as less than human.

I stopped eating pork more than fifteen years ago. Recently I was visiting family, and my sister was preparing dinner for her family. Fried pork chops was on the menu! The aroma of the pork chops was pleasing to my sense of smell, and I remembered how pleasing pork chops were to my sense of taste. Because the pork chops had such a powerful appeal, I lusted after those chops in my heart!

Anger

Anger is an intense feeling of rage or displeasure. Anger is a natural reaction; even Jesus got angry at times: "He looked around at them in anger and, deeply distressed at their stubborn hearts, said to the man, 'Stretch out your hand.' He stretched it out, and his hand was completely restored" (Mark 3:5). God is angry from time to time: "The anger of the Lord burned against them, and he left them" (Num. 12:9).

Although anger is a natural reaction, the spiritual person is expected to be disciplined enough not to act out of anger. When we act out of anger, we often sin. Anger becomes a problem when we allow it to stay with us for too long. Paul suggests that twenty-four hours is too long for one to be consumed with anger. The spiritual person is not to allow the sun to set upon his anger.

We must deal with anger quickly; if we don't, we give the devil an opportunity to establish a foot-hold in our lives. Sustained anger becomes a totally consuming force. Anger pollutes our thinking and causes our thoughts to be rendered impure. When we are consumed with anger, we cannot know the peace of God.

Greed

Greed is an excessive or rapacious desire, especially for wealth or possessions. Of all the contaminants that pollute our thinking and cause our thoughts to become impure, greed is the most seductive. Greed is so subtle that it overtakes people without their awareness. That's why Jesus said: "Watch out! Be on your guard against all kinds of greed; a man's life does not consist in the abundance of his possessions" (Luke 12:15).

The context of this passage in Luke is very interesting. A young man came to Jesus and appealed to His authority as a community rabbi to render a legally binding decision on his behalf in a dispute he had with his older brother. The father had died; all of the father's possessions were left to the older brother. The older brother was supposed to divide the inheritance with his mother and siblings, but in this case, the older brother refused to divide the inheritance with his brother. The wronged brother came to Jesus and requested that He use His rabbinical authority to force the older brother to divide the inheritance. Despite the surface validity of this request, Jesus rebuked him and implied that he was greedy, because he did not need anything. Those obsessed with greed constantly seek to acquire more and more. Our culture celebrates greed. Think of the Fortune 500 president who negotiates with his company annual salaries of hundreds of millions of dollars. We celebrate the athlete who refuses to practice with his team because his fifty-million-dollar contract is not enough; he holds out until he gets six million more. The war in

Iraq, the drug trade, the inflated gas prices, and the recent corporate scandals are all symptoms of greed. To think constantly about acquiring more than I need pollutes my thinking, makes my thoughts impure, and keeps me from ever knowing the peace of God.

Laziness

Lazy people are disinclined to do what they are supposed to do when they are supposed to do it. They often suffer because of their reluctance to work. The book of Proverbs speaks most pointedly to the problem of laziness and its consequences:

- "Being lazy will make you poor, but hard work will make you rich" (Prov. 10:4).
- "Hard work will give you power; being lazy will make you a slave" (Prov. 10:28).
- "If you are lazy, you will meet difficulty everywhere" (Prov. 15:19).
- "A lazy person will think he is smarter than seven men who can give good reasons for their opinions" (Prov. 26:16).

Poverty in itself cannot separate us from experiencing the peace of God. But when poverty is caused by laziness, it often prevents us from experiencing the peace of God. For example, there was a young man who had a good job in the manufacturing sector. He was fortunate to have this job, because his credentials and work experience were far below the requirements for it. But he was lazy. Every day he would leave his post for an hour and sneak to a small room to take a nap. Over time, his supervisor discovered his secret, followed him to his daily hideaway, and caught him sleeping on the job. He was fired immediately. Consequently, he lost his house, car, and health insurance.

He came to the church several times for help, and the church helped him until he began asking for help on a regular basis. When the church stopped giving him handouts and started trying to help him find a job, he got angry and left the church. He never joined another church and blamed God and his family. Proverbs 10:4 says, "Being lazy will make you poor."

Being lazy will also make you a slave. I encourage young people to work hard at whatever they decide to do. If in school, study hard; if in sports, business, music, or entertainment, work hard. If you are lazy, you are going to end up slaving for someone else.

If you are lazy, you will meet with difficulty everywhere. If you are lazy at work, your supervisor is going to give you a difficult time. If you are lazy at home, your house will be dirty, you'll pay your bills late, and you'll most likely have arguments with those in your household. You are going to have problems at church, because the preacher is going to talk about discipline, service, and commitment, and you are going to be offended. You are going to have a difficult time in relationships, because the other person is going to get tired of doing everything while you do nothing.

Lazy people think they are smarter than others. They spend a lot of time making up lies and excuses to avoid doing work. Lazy people are experts at blaming others because they couldn't do their jobs. They often cloud issues to take the focus off themselves when the issue was created because of their laziness. That's why Proverbs 10:26 warns, "Never get a lazy person to do something for you; he will be as irritating as vinegar on your teeth or smoke in your eyes."

Laziness pollutes our thinking and causes our thoughts to be impure.

Chapter 8

Think on Those Things That Are Beautiful
Philippians 4:8

What is beauty? Beauty cannot be defined, because it is subjective. Beauty then is an idea that we carry around in our consciousness. It is a template that we have in our minds; when something in the outside world fits that internal *beauty* template, we call it "beautiful." This internal template of beauty is not fixed or static, but ever changing; it is flexible and pliable, based upon the conditions of our lives.

A wise old guru had been sitting upon a hard rock on a mountain peak for many years. One day a man reached the top of the mountain so that he could receive guidance and wisdom from the guru. The first question the seeker asked the guru was, "Sir, what makes for true happiness?" to which the guru replied, "A nice, soft pillow." A nice soft pillow made for happiness and beauty for the guru.

Life's conditions are constantly reshaping our beauty template. My younger brother used to have a clear mental template of how he wanted his ideal woman to look. He finally found a woman who met all his criteria of beauty. The first few days of dating were perfection. But she gave him such a hard time for so long that after they broke up, he avoided women who looked anything like her. In fact, he married a young lady who is the total opposite physical type of what he used to desire.

Kahlil Gibran writes the following about beauty:

And a poet said, Speak to us of Beauty.
And he answered:
Where shall you seek beauty,
and how shall you find her unless she herself
be your way and your guide?
And how shall you speak of her except
she be the Weaver of your speech?

The aggrieved and the injured say,
"Beauty is kind and gentle."
The passionate say, "No, beauty is a
thing of might and dread."

The tired and the weary say,
"Beauty is of soft whispering."
But the restless say,
"We have heard her shouting
among the mountain. . . . "
At night the watchmen of the city say,
"Beauty shall rise with the dawn from the East."
And at noontide the toilers and the
wayfarers say, "We have seen her leaning over
the earth from the windows of the sunset."

In the winter says the snowbound,
"She shall come with the spring
leaping upon the hills."
And in summer heat the reapers say,
"We have seen her dancing with the
autumn leaves, and we saw a drift of
snow in her hair."

All these things have you said of beauty,
Yet in all you spoke of her but of needs
        unsatisfied,

And beauty is not a need or an ecstasy.
It is not an empty hand stretched forth,
But rather a heart enflamed and a soul
        enchanted.[2]

Whatever enflames *your* heart and enchants *your*
soul is beauty. For the injured, it is kindness. For the

[2] Kahlil Gibran, *The Prophet*. New York: Alfred A Knopf, 1985. p. 74

passionate, it is might. For the weary, it is soft whispers. For the night watchman, it is the dawning of a new day. For the wayfarers, it is the setting of the sun. For the snowbound, beauty is the coming of summer. Yet for the summer reapers, beauty is the dawning of autumn, because, for them, these are the things that enflame the heart and enchant the soul.

Saint Thomas Aquinas once wrote, "The beautiful is that which pleases us upon being seen." And Aquinas does not merely mean to see something from a distance, but rather he means to experience that something for yourself. If I receive pleasure from one of my thoughts, that particular thought is beautiful. Beauty is relative and, indeed, in the eye of the beholder. What's beautiful to me may not be beautiful to anyone else.

There is beauty in every situation in life. Rather than focus on the ugly aspect of a given situation, why not simply acknowledge that the ugly is there but focus on the beauty of the situation instead?

Two biblical characters experienced a series of misfortunes. Joseph focused on the beauty that was hidden in the tragedy and ended up at peace, happy, and productive. Naomi, the other character, focused on the ugly dimensions of her situation and became bitter, cold, and mean.

In Genesis 37, the story of Joseph teaches us that if we will focus on the beauty in every difficult situation, we will be empowered, not only to endure the situation, but also to endure with an attitude of grace and power.

Joseph's jealous brothers stripped him of his coat of many colors given to him by his father and threw him into a pit. They dipped the coat in blood, returned it to his father, and told him that Joseph had been attacked and killed by wild animals.

Joseph was then taken out of the pit by merchants and sold into slavery in Egypt. He worked faithfully for Potiphar. Joseph resisted Potiphar's wife's sexual advances, but she accused him of attempted rape. Joseph was then imprisoned.

While in prison, Joseph did favors for the inmates, who promised not to forget about him upon their release; but when they were paroled, they forgot all about Joseph. Eventually, because God was with Joseph, he was promoted to the top position in Egypt, second only to Pharaoh.

What if Joseph had spent all of his time focusing on the harm that his brothers had done to him? It is not likely that he would have been likable enough for Potiphar to hire him and promote him to the status to which he ascended.

What you constantly think about continuously expands. That is, the more you think about a certain thing, the more you tend to think about it. If you constantly think about the cruel things that others have done to you, you will ultimately become a cruel person, because what you constantly think about expand into action. But when someone has sinned against you, focus on the beauty of God's divine plan unfolding in your life and realize that God is using that wrongdoer to fulfill His beautiful plan for your life. Romans 8:28 is my favorite passage: "And we know that God's works all things together for our good."

Although Joseph was falsely accused and imprisoned, he neither denounced anyone nor complained about anything. Joseph had enough sense to know to never curse a situation that he wanted to change. Why add negativity to a situation that's already negative? That will make the situation even more difficult to change. That's why Jesus said, "Bless those who curse you." When I curse those who curse me, I am only adding more negative energy to the situation. But when I bless those who curse me, I am nullifying the negative energy by countering it with positive energy.

When Joseph finally reached the height that God had intended for him from the beginning, he uttered these words to his trembling brothers standing before him, letting us know that he saw the beauty in every unfortunate situation in his life: "You meant it for evil, but God meant it for good."

Naomi also had misfortunes in her life. She lived in Bethlehem but moved to Moab with her husband. There they started their family. They had two sons who grew up to marry Moabite women. Naomi's husband died; then both her sons died. After many painful years, she returned to Bethlehem.

When the people recognized that Naomi had returned, they celebrated. But she was so embittered by life that she demanded that the townspeople call her "Bitter," not Naomi, because in her view, the Lord had dealt bitterly with her. The beauty of God's purpose unfolding in her life was that her daughter-in-law Ruth returned to Bethlehem, met Boaz, married him, and had a son named Obed. Obed, in turn, became the father of Jesse, who became the father of King David, the distant relative of our Lord Jesus Christ.

There is beauty in any and all situations. Think on the things that are beautiful.

Chapter 9

Think on Those Things
That Are of Value
Philippians 4:8

This virtue has more English translations than any of the other virtues. The King James Version translates it "good report." The Revised Standard Version has it "good reputation." The New International Version's rendition is "admirable." The New Revised Standard Version says "commendable." However, the Bible in Basic English embraces all of the above by rendering it "whatsoever things are of value."

There are some thoughts that are of value to you and thoughts that are of no value at all and sometimes even destructive. Paul said to fill your minds with thoughts that are of value to you. Whenever you find yourself dwelling on a specific thought, ask yourself: What value does this thought have for me? Does this thought bring me into the peace of God, or is it causing me fear, anxiety, stress, and frustration? Most of our thoughts are of past happenings or of events anticipated in the future. Very little, if any, of our thoughts focus on the present. Notice the content of your next conversation and notice how much of the conversational content is on past events or on the future, and how little time is spent talking about the present moment. The content of our conversation is a reflection of our thinking. If most of our conversation is about the past or future, then most of our thinking is about the past or future.

Focusing your thinking on your personal past or future has very little, if any, value at all. In fact, focusing your thoughts on the past often creates regret, guilt, or anger. And focusing your thoughts on the future usually creates stress, fear, and worriment. These negative emotions move you further away from experiencing the peace of God.

To regret is to feel a deep sense of sorrow over a decision you made in the past. Many of us are living in regret. Living in regret robs you of the peace of God that can be experienced only in the present. I hear people complain, "I regret having dropped out of school," or "I regret I had babies so early in life," or "I regret I took that job rather than getting married," or "I regret I married the person I did," or "I regret I got a divorce," or "I regret I didn't take that job when I had the chance." It is impossible to simultaneously live in the present and live with regret over some decision in the past. There are only two options: You can either live in the present without regret, or you can live locked in the past by your regret. And if you are not in the present, you are missing God.

Focusing your thoughts on the past also exposes you to anger. If you are angry right now, is it because of what is happening to you right now, in this present moment? Probably not, because nobody is likely doing anything to you while you are reading this book at this very moment. If you are angry, it is likely because of something that has happened in the past. There is nothing you can do to change your past. So you must let go of that anger by leaving it in the past where it belongs and not giving it a place in your present.

My son and I went to the Bahamas for spring break. I watched him as he rode the Jet Ski. As he sped across the water on the Jet Ski, it left a stream of white foamy water behind, called the wake. It is not the wake that empowered the Jet Ski to move forward, but it was the present moment energy in the engine. There is no power or value in the wake; similarly, the power of His presence reside only in the present.

Many people focus their thoughts on future events, which has virtually no value either. I don't mean to imply that we should not plan for future events and sometimes even visualize how we would like for them to turn out. To the contrary, this is very healthy. In fact, to use the present moment to plan for the future is wise usage of your present.

However, there is a vast difference between using your present moment to plan for the future and leaving the present and living in the future. To sit down and calculate how much college tuition is going to cost for your kids and setting up a savings plan for that purpose is planning for the future. On the other hand, worrying about inflation and whether your savings plan will provide enough to cover total expenses, fretting over what will happen if the stock market crashes, worrying what you will do if you lose your job, or obsessing over a million other things that can go wrong is living in the future. It creates stress and anxiety and prevents you from living in the present and knowing the peace of God. Paul said to think on those things that are of value. The present moment has value to the Christian because it is only in the present moment that we can know the peace of God.

Chapter 10

Those Things That Deserve Praise
Philippians 4:8

There are at least five Greek words for the English word *praise*. One of the Greek words used in the New Testament for the word *praise* is *ainos*. *Ainos* is exclusively used when referring to the praise of God. However, the word used for praise in this text is *epainos*, which has to do with the act of expressing approval, admiration or commendation.

If you are to know the peace of God, you must give commendation, admiration, and laudation where they are due—even if they are due to yourself. How often do you commend or admire yourself because of some good thing you have done? Self-admiration is one of the most difficult things for many Christians to engage in. We often mistake self-admiration with haughtiness. As Christians, we are taught the evils of pride and haughtiness. The book of Proverbs 16:18

says, "Pride goes before a fall and a haughty spirit before destruction." It is the meek who shall inherit the earth and the humble who shall be exalted.

Self-admiration, however, should never be confused with haughtiness. Haughtiness means "disdainfully proud," "snobbish," "scornfully arrogant," and "supercilious." But self-admiration is to feel good about yourself, to pat yourself on the back, or even to reward yourself because of some noble act you have performed. You were created to feel good about yourself when you perform good deeds.

A study was conducted to measure the level of serotonin in the human body when an individual performed a good deed for someone else. (Serotonin is the chemical produced in the brain that provides the human body with peace, bliss, and even sleep. In fact, many of the antidepressant drugs are designed to stimulate the production of serotonin.) The study found that both the person who does a good deed for someone else and the recipient of that good deed experience increased serotonin levels.

God has physiologically created us to feel good about our good deeds. So, don't fight it! You were created to celebrate your good deeds. When you buy a struggling family a week's worth of groceries with love as a motive, you have earned the right to feel good about yourself and admire what you have done. When, out of genuine love and compassion, you take a homeless person home with you and let her get out of the cold for a while, allow her to take a nice hot bath, wash her clothes, get her a hot meal, and give her a few dollars before she leaves, you've done a good deed and should admire yourself and feel good about it. That's worthy of self-celebration. When you go to the hospital to minister to the sick to lift someone's spirits, you've performed a noble act that will make you feel good about yourself.

If you have poor self-esteem, the best way to eliminate it is to perform a noble act for another. You must do something good that will make *you* feel good about yourself, rather than depending on others to affirm you to make you feel good. In Psalm 18, David mentions his good deeds and even attributes his good fortune and divine favor to them:

> The LORD dealt with me according to my righteousness; according to the cleanness of my hands he rewarded me. For I have kept the ways of the LORD, and have not wickedly departed from my God. For all his rules were before me, and his statutes I did not put away from me. I was blameless before him, and I kept myself from my guilt. So the LORD has rewarded me according to my righteousness, according to the cleanness of my hands in his sight. With the merciful you show yourself merciful; with the blameless man you show yourself blameless; with the purified you show yourself pure.
>
> —Psalm 18

Make sure, however, that your motive is based on self-admiration and not on an attempt to gain admiration from others. Jesus advises us not to brag about our good deeds but encourages us to do them in secrecy. In fact, God will reward you openly if your left hand does not know what your right hand is doing. The open reward that Christ promises will not necessarily be tangible; it could be something better—such as the peace that you seek in your life.

Thinking about the good things you have done will help you experience the peace of God. Too much of our time, though, is spent thinking about the bad things we have done. The feelings of remorse and guilt over past failures will rob you of God's peace.

The Bible reminds us often that we are already forgiven of our sins. I enjoy the Bible because it is the story about God's love and His forgiveness. The Old Testament is full of passages about forgiveness. Psalm 103:2-4 says, "Praise the Lord, O my soul, and forget not all his benefits—who forgives all your sins." Micah 7:18 says, "Who is a God like you, who pardons sin and forgives the transgression?" Psalms 85:2 says, "You forgave the iniquity of your people and covered all their sins." Isaiah 1:18 says, " 'Come now, let us reason together,' " says the Lord. 'Though your sins are like scarlet, they shall be as white as snow; though they are red as crimson, they shall be like wool.' " Isaiah 38:17 states, "In your love you kept me from the pit of destruction; you have put all my sins behind your back." Isaiah 43:25 tells us, "I am he who blots out your transgressions and remembers your sins no more." Isaiah 44:22 says, "I have swept away your offenses like a cloud, your sins like the morning mist."

These messages continue through the New Testament. Matthew 1:21 says, "[Mary] will give birth to a son, and you are to give him the name Jesus, because he will save his people from their sins." Ephesians 1:7 says, "In him we have redemption through his blood, the forgiveness of sins." Hebrews 10:12 says, "But when Jesus had offered for all time one sacrifice for sins, he sat down at the right hand of God."

If you feel guilty about your sins even after God has forgiven you, your guilt is not caused by the convicting ministry of the Holy Spirit, but by the accusatory activity of the devil, because the Bible says that he is the accuser of the brethren. Since we have been forgiven by God, forgive yourself and begin to celebrate the good deeds you have done.

Admire and celebrate the good of others. To commend the good in someone else does not diminish you—it adds peace and joy to your life. You do yourself a favor by lauding the good of others. Many cannot celebrate the good in others because they are living under the tyranny of the ego. The ego will not allow many people to commend the good in others because to do so would make them feel inferior to others.

For example, if Ms. Weatherbee is a great singer with an oversized ego, she will refuse to acknowledge the talents of Ms. Beeweather, who is also a great singer. Ego tells Ms. Weatherbee that to commend Ms. Beeweather is to condemn herself, but to condemn Ms. Beeweather is to commend herself. So when Ms. Weatherbee sings, she is not singing for the joy of singing, but to compete with Ms. Beeweather. And when Ms. Beeweather sings, Ms. Weatherbee listens for flaws and mistakes so that she can have reason to condemn her "rival." Ms. Weatherbee will find it difficult to experience the peace of God, even when she is singing and using the gift God gave her.

When you detach from ego, you are free to commend and enjoy the good in others. You can celebrate when a co-worker makes the most sales, receives a promotion, or is named "Employee of the Year," because you have learned how to look for what is praiseworthy in others and appreciate it.

Conclusion

The most important word that Paul uses in Philippians 4:8 is the term *think*. He uses this verb in the presence tense. He is attempting to keep his audience in the present. Paul understands that the peace of God can be experienced only in the present. Paul does not encourage his readers to think of future events or past experiences, but rather encourages them to allow the thoughts of these virtues to find expression in the present.